NEW FOREST COUNTRY BY CAR

INCLUDING . . .

Badbury Rings, Beaulieu Abbey, Boldre, Breamore, Buckler's Hard, Burley, Christchurch, Cranborne, Fordingbridge, Lymington, Ringwood, Rockbourne, Rufus Stone, Salisbury, Sway, and Wimborne Minster.

This guide book contains exact but simple directions enabling you to explore the New Forest and the small towns and villages of the Bournemouth area, most of which lie hidden between the main roads.

The 'Main Circle' Route (Maps 1 – 11) shown on the Key Map covers 130 miles, most of which are over quiet roads through pleasant countryside. This route can be approached from Bournemouth, Southampton, or the other surrounding towns. You will find that the strip maps show the A roads approaching from the towns, thus giving an easy link with 'civilization'.

The 'Main Circle' route (Maps 1 – 11) is far too long for a leisurely day's journey, and we have therefore included 'link routes' to give you better coverage of the Forest, and to break the route up into smaller circles. A 'South Circle' could consist of Maps 1 – 2 – 12 – 13 – 14 and part of 11; an 'East Circle' could consist of Maps 1 – 2 – 3 – 4 – 5 – 6 – 13 – 14; and a 'West Circle', by going north on the A 338 to Breamore (Map 7) and then using Maps 7 – 8 – 9 – 10 – 11. We have also included a 'quiet road' link to Salisbury on Map 15, as it lies so close to the Forest.

It should be stressed that each route, being circular, may be started at any point, and that a break can be made anywhere should you wish to visit a nearby town for lunch, or to stay in a hotel for the night. You will find directions for doing this clearly marked on the borders of the strip maps, and although mileages are not shown, these can easily be worked out by reference to the Key Map opposite.

HOW TO USE YOUR BOOK ON THE ROUTE

Each double page makes up a complete picture of the country ahead of you. On the left you will find a one inch to the mile strip map, with the route marked by a series of dashes. Direction is always from top to bottom, so that the map may be looked at in conjunction with the 'directions to the driver', with which it is cross referenced by a letter itemising each junction point. This enables the driver to have exact guidance every time an opportunity for changing direction occurs, even if it is only 'Keep straight, not left!'

With mileage intervals shown, the driver should even have warning when to expect these 'moments of decision', and if a sign post exists we have used this to help you, with the 'Follow sign marked...' column. However re-signing is always in progress, and this may lead to slight differences in sign marking in some cases... So beware of freshly erected signs.

We have also included a description of the towns and villages through which you will pass, together with some photographs to illustrate the route.

To gain full enjoyment from these journeys, be prepared to leave your car as often as possible. We have found you quiet roads through the Forest and over the downlands to the west, but to absorb the real atmosphere of this splendid area, switch off that engine and idle away the hours, whether it be on a deserted shoreline, in the shade of the great forest oaks, or along a quiet village street... it is all yours to enjoy.

Compiled by PETER and HELEN TITCHMARSH
Photography by ALAN and PETER TITCHMARSH

MAP 1

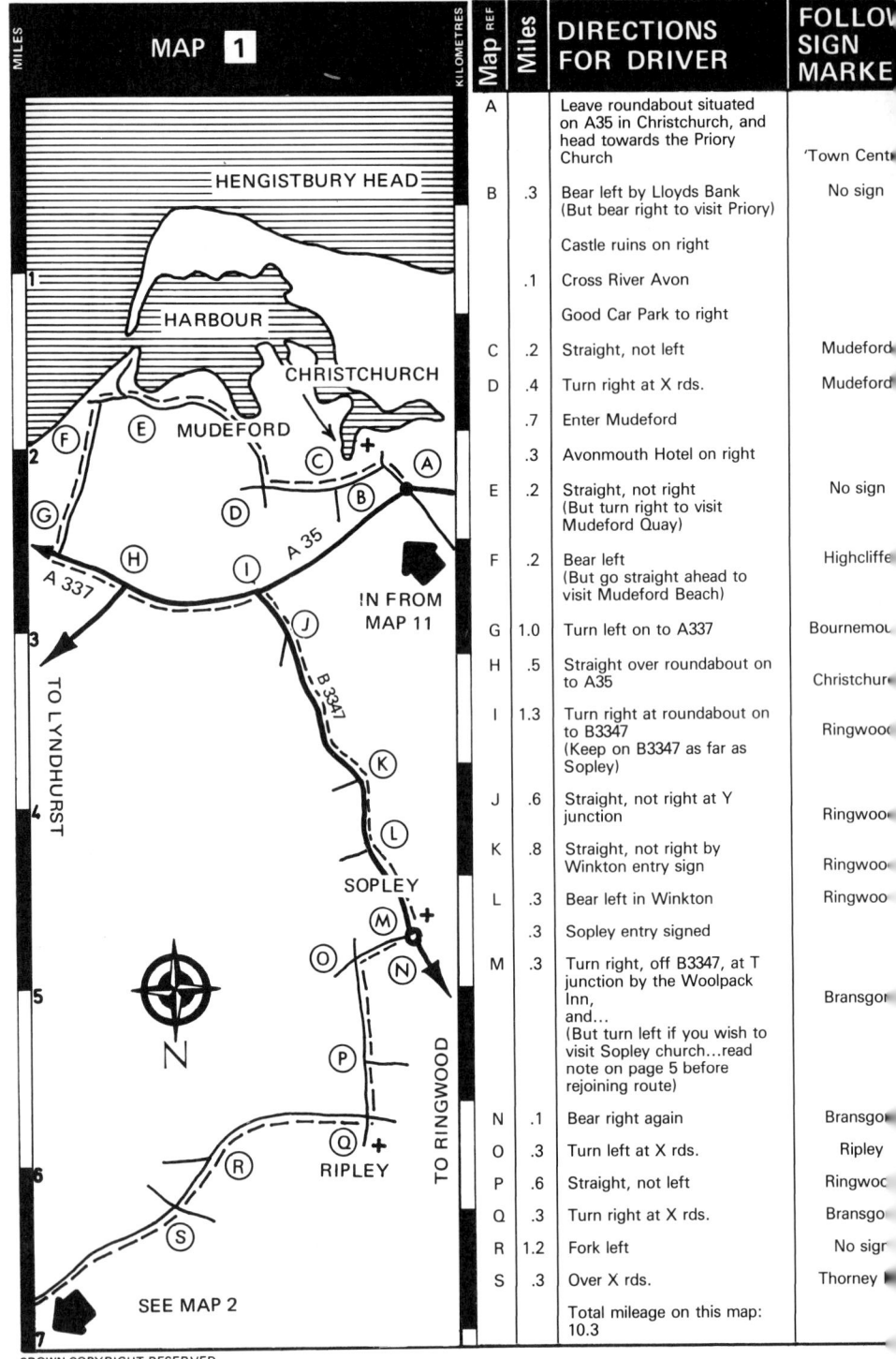

Map REF	Miles	DIRECTIONS FOR DRIVER	FOLLOW SIGN MARKED
A		Leave roundabout situated on A35 in Christchurch, and head towards the Priory Church	'Town Centre'
B	.3	Bear left by Lloyds Bank (But bear right to visit Priory)	No sign
		Castle ruins on right	
	.1	Cross River Avon	
		Good Car Park to right	
C	.2	Straight, not left	Mudeford
D	.4	Turn right at X rds.	Mudeford
	.7	Enter Mudeford	
	.3	Avonmouth Hotel on right	
E	.2	Straight, not right (But turn right to visit Mudeford Quay)	No sign
F	.2	Bear left (But go straight ahead to visit Mudeford Beach)	Highcliffe
G	1.0	Turn left on to A337	Bournemouth
H	.5	Straight over roundabout on to A35	Christchurch
I	1.3	Turn right at roundabout on to B3347 (Keep on B3347 as far as Sopley)	Ringwood
J	.6	Straight, not right at Y junction	Ringwood
K	.8	Straight, not right by Winkton entry sign	Ringwood
L	.3	Bear left in Winkton	Ringwood
	.3	Sopley entry signed	
M	.3	Turn right, off B3347, at T junction by the Woolpack Inn, and... (But turn left if you wish to visit Sopley church...read note on page 5 before rejoining route)	Bransgore
N	.1	Bear right again	Bransgore
O	.3	Turn left at X rds.	Ripley
P	.6	Straight, not left	Ringwood
Q	.3	Turn right at X rds.	Bransgore
R	1.2	Fork left	No sign
S	.3	Over X rds.	Thorney
		Total mileage on this map: 10.3	

SEE MAP 2

CROWN COPYRIGHT RESERVED

PLACES OF INTEREST ON THE ROUTE

Christchurch

Surrounded on three sides by suburban and holiday developments, the small town of Christchurch has, by some miracle, preserved a pleasing character all its own. It is situated on a narrow strip of land between the rivers Stour and Avon, immediately above the point where they empty into the broad waters of Christchurch Harbour.

The Harbour is overlooked by one of England's finest churches below cathedral status, the wonderful Christchurch Priory. It was originally built by Bishop Flambard of Durham, Chancellor and friend of William Rufus, in the 11th and early 12th century, and the massive nave and transepts, and the beautiful stair turret outside the north transept bear witness to the Norman genius for the combination of strength and beauty. It is impossible here to do justice to the splendours of the Priory, but do not overlook the wonderful 14th century reredos with Jesse at its foot, the four beautiful chantry chapels, (especially that of the Countess of Salisbury), and the delightful carvings on the choir stalls.

Between the Priory and the Avon bridges are the scanty remains of a Norman castle, with a ruined keep on a grassy mound, and beside the river, the Castle Hall, usually referred to as the Constable's House. Not over exciting perhaps, but these ruins are delightfully sited amongst well kept gardens, and are an open invitation to walk down beside the river, towards Christchurch Quay, with its views across the harbour to Hengistbury Head (See Mudeford, below).

Mudeford

Quiet holiday resort with a sprinkling of Georgian and early Victorian houses, and fading memories of Coleridge and Walter Scott, both of whom stayed here for a time. It was also from Mudeford that a certain Squire Tregonwell drove in his carriage sometime in 1810 and lighted upon Bourne Chine, a deserted sandy shore on the heathland a few miles westward and decided to build himself a house here....thus taking the first unconscious step in the establishment of Bournemouth.

Mudeford has an excellent beach, but it is best known for its quay, which looks out across the narrow channel at the entrance to Christchurch Harbour. Park your car here and stroll on the quay, take the ferry across to the sand spit and walk across to Hengistbury Head, or simply sit and watch the comings and goings of the ever active dinghy sailors on the harbour shore.

Sopley

Pleasant village, rather disturbed by traffic, with a hospitable little inn, The Woolpack. The church lies well back from the road and is prettily sited on a little knoll overlooking the mill, with brimming sluices and the Avon water meadows beyond. (Good wild duck spotting in winter time.)

continued on page 5

1. Christchurch Priory
2. Stair Turret, Christchurch Priory 
3. Fishing at Christchurch 
4. At Mudeford Quay 
5. On Mudeford Beach

MAP 2

Map labels

- BARBUSH CAR PARK
- BURLEY
- CAR PARKS
- GOATSPEN CAMPING AREA AND CAR PARK
- TO CHRISTCHURCH
- A 35
- TO LYNDHURST
- YEW TREE BOTTOM CAR PARK
- LONG SLADE BOTTOM CAR PARKS
- SETTHORNS CAMPING AREA
- SWAY TOWER
- TO BROCKENHURST
- A 337
- TO LYMINGTON
- SEE MAP 3

Directions

Map Ref	Miles	Directions for Driver	Follow Sign Marked
A	1.4	Turn left at X rds., after crossing cattle grid, and entering Forest area	Burley
		Lovely open country with extensive views	
	1.2	Cross disused railway line	
		Burbush Car Park on right	
	.1	Enter Burley	
B	1.0	Straight, not left, and immediately…	Ringwood
		Fork right up hill	Brockenhurst
	.2	Car Parks on left and right	
C	.6	Straight, not left	No sign
D	.1	Over X rds. keeping on wider road	Brockenhurst
	.7	Goatspen Car Park and Camping Area on right	
E	.5	Straight, not right, and…	
		Under bridge beneath A35	
F	.2	Straight, not right	Brockenhurst
G	1.2	Straight, not right	Sway
	.4	Yew Tree Bottom Car Park over to right	
H	.2	Fork right and bear right	Sway
	.2	Long Slade Car Parks on left	
	.4	Setthorns Camping Area on right	
	.2	Cross disused railway line	
I	.5	Straight, not right	Lymington
J	.9	Over X rds., crossing B3055	Boldre
		Sway Tower visible over to right	
K	1.3	Turn right on to A337	Lymington
		(BUT TO LINK WITH MAP 12, POINT A, TURN LEFT ON TO A337 AND DRIVE 2 MILES, INTO BROCKENHURST)	
L	.1	Turn sharp left (Watch for this with great care)	'Lower Sandy Lane'
M	.2	Straight, not left	No sign
		Total mileage on this map: 11.6	

CROWN COPYRIGHT RESERVED

PLACES OF INTEREST ON THE ROUTE

Sopley *continued from page 3*

Lilac and flowering trees overhung the churchyard path when we called, and although the exterior has been much restored, we found the interior to be full of character and interest. It has high arcading, with two interesting corbel heads, two 13th century monuments on either side of the doorway, whose swathed figures have a strangely 20th century feeling about them. Do not miss the attractive linenfold panelling beneath the tower.

(N.B. BE SURE TO TURN LEFT INTO THE ONE-WAY SYSTEM AT THE WOOLPACK BEFORE REJOINING THE ROUTE. YOU WILL THEN HAVE TO TAKE FIRST RIGHT AND FIRST LEFT TO ARRIVE BACK AT MAP 1, POINT N.)

Burley

One of the few villages in the New Forest, Burley is attractively situated, but contains little of interest earlier than the 19th century. There are, typically of the period, rhododendrons and mock half timbering in profusion, but gift shops, restaurants and hotels are also in evidence and the 'Forest' atmosphere is enhanced by riders from the nearby stables, and the inevitable ponies, all of whom must rely on your careful driving (PLEASE!).

Sway Tower

This prominent landmark lies about a mile to the south of our route between Points I and J. It is 218 feet high and was built in 1879 by a judge retired from India, as a mausoleum for himself. It was also intended to demonstrate the effectiveness of concrete, a material which was still a novelty at the time. It is not open to the public.

Boldre (See Page 6)

A scattered, woody village lying to the immediate east of the Boldre, or Lymington River, with a long, low thatched inn.....The Fleur De Lys, and several other 'pretty' cottages. The church lies well to the north of the village and is reached by a road winding up from the stream beneath the trees. The top half of its squat tower was built as late as 1697 and is of attractive mellow brick. From outside, the great spread of the low pitched roof over the nave and aisles resembles a tithe barn and there is a correspondingly spacious atmosphere within. The building dates from about 1150 and there is Norman arcading to the south aisle. Do not miss the handsome 17th century wall tablet to John Kempe (1652), and the memorial to William Gilpin. Gilpin was rector of Boldre from 1777 to 1804 and author of 'Forest Sketches' and several other topographical works. In the porch one can read the sad story of H.M.S. Hood, the battleship which was sunk in May 1941 with such tragic loss of life.

1. Corbel Head in Sopley Church

2. The Queen's Head, Burley

3. Open Forest beyond Point H

4. Boldre Church

MAP 3

Map REF	Miles	DIRECTIONS FOR DRIVER	FOLLOW SIGN MARKED
A	.3	Fork left	No sign
B	.1	Over small X rds., bearing right	No sign
C	.2	Over X rds. with care	Boldre Church
D	.4	Straight, not right	No sign
	.1	Boldre Church on left	
E	.7	Turn right at T junction	Pilley Hill
	.1	Fleur de Lys Inn on left	
F	.2	Turn left at T junction	Vicar's Hill
G	.3	Straight, not left	No sign
H	.2	Fork right by oak tree	No sign
I	.9	Straight, not left. On to B3054	No sign
J	.1	Straight, not right. Off B3054 (But turn right to visit Lymington, which is recommended)	Sowley
		Attractive creek here; especially at high tide	
	.5	Isle of Wight Ferry Terminal on right	
		Isle of Wight now visible across the water	
K	.1	Straight, not left	No sign
L	.2	Fork left, beyond Elmers Court, keeping on wider road	No sign
M	.2	Straight, not left, keeping on wider road	No sign
N	.3	Over X rds. by lodge and gates	No sign
O	.6	Straight, not left, by school	No sign
P	.7	Turn right by cottages beyond cattle grid	Sowley
Q	.2	Bear left (But fork right for ½ mile to visit the shore at Tanners Lane)	Sowley
	.9	Sowley Pond on left	
R	1.2	Turn right at T junction	Beaulieu
S	.1	Straight, not left	Buckler's Hard
	1.3	Hamlet of St. Leonards, with remains of vast barn belonging to Beaulieu Abbey on left	
	.1	Ruined chapel over to left, close to the Grange	
T	.4	Turn right at T junction	Buckler's Hard
		Total mileage on this map: 10.4	

CROWN COPYRIGHT RESERVED

PLACES OF INTEREST ON THE ROUTE

Boldre (See Page 5)

Vicars Hill
At point H is the mellow brick rectory where William Gilpin lived and worked (See Boldre, page 5). There are pleasant glimpses of the Isle of Wight from here.

Lymington
Although off our route, Lymington is well worth the short diversion. At high tide the creek is alive with boats dancing at their moorings, and there are fine views across the Solent to the Isle of Wight. If possible you should park your car in the town and walk down brightly coloured Quay Street, with its Georgian bow fronts, and explore the quays, now devoted to sailing and pleasure boating. Return the same way and climb beyond Quay Street to the busy High Street, which is dominated by the church of St. Thomas with its tall cupola. The church dates back to the Norman period but within, an 18th century atmosphere prevails, with galleries supported by Tuscan columns. Do not miss the Courtenay Chapel or the monument to Charles Colebourn by Rysbrack (1747).

Tanners Lane
Leads to saltings from where there are fine views across to the Isle of Wight. This is a splendidly remote place out of season, and an excellent place for bird watching in the winter months.

Sowley Pond
A most attractive stretch of water surrounded by woodlands, but only separated from the saltings by half a mile of marsh. In winter it is much visited by waterfowl, and in summer by terns and herons. Sowley Pond is private, but there is good bird watching from the road.

St. Leonards
This was a grange of Beaulieu Abbey (See page 9), and close beside it stand the ruins of a small 13th century chapel. However it is the remains of the vast tithe barn in the farmyard on our left that is of most interest. This was originally no less than 216 feet long and must have dwarfed Beaulieu's other tithe barn at Great Coxwell in Berkshire, which is itself 150 feet long.

Additional Reading. The Forestry Commission publish a guide entitled 'Explore the New Forest', an inexpensive map entitled 'New Forest Map Guide', and various leaflets including ones on the Bolderwood Walks, the Ornamental Drives, the Ober Water Walk, and Amphibians and Reptiles. 'The Countryside of the New Forest', published by Jarrolds Colour Publications, is an excellently written and illustrated guide for those wishing to learn more about the natural history of this fascinating area.

---

1. Quay Street, Lymington

2. Shoreline at Tanners Lane

3. Sowley Pond

4. Tithe Barn, St. Leonards

MAP 4

Map REF	Miles	DIRECTIONS FOR DRIVER	FOLLOW SIGN MARKED
A	.7	Turn left at T junction at entry to Buckler's Hard. (But turn right for car park)	Beaulieu
B	.6	Straight, not left at T junction	Beaulieu
C	1.2	Bear right at T junction	Beaulieu
	.1	Fine barn on left	
D	.5	Bear right on to B3054	No sign
	.2	Turn right at T junction	Beaulieu Village
	.1	Beaulieu entry signed	
		Palace House over to left	
E	.1	Turn left by the Montagu Arms	Hythe
	.1	Beaulieu River creek on right	
F	1.1	Turn right, off B3054, and immediately...	Fawley
		Turn right again, by the Royal Oak Inn	
		Fawley Refinery visible over to left	
	.8	Over cattle grid, leaving the forest area, at the Otterwood Gate	
G	1.7	Straight, not right	No sign
	.1	Entrance to Exbury Gardens on right	
H	.1	Straight, not left	Inchmere
I	.8	Sharp turn left	No sign
J	1.2	Straight, not left	Langley
K	.7	Arrive Lepe Beach Country Park and TURNABOUT	
J	.7	Bear right	Exbury
L	1.3	Bear left at T junction	Exbury
	.2	Re-enter Exbury	
H2	.1	Turn right at T junction (Now re-tracing our route as far as Beaulieu, Point E)	Beaulieu
F2	2.6	Turn left and left again, rejoining B3054	No sign
	.7	Re-enter Beaulieu	
E2	.6	Turn right at T junction by the Montagu Arms	Lyndhurst
	.1	Turn right on to wider road...the B3056	Lyndhurst
	.5	Entrance to Motor Museum, Palace House, and Beaulieu Abbey on right	
M	.6	Turn right at T junction, off B3056	Totton
	.9	Northgate Car Park on left	
		Total mileage on this map: 18.4	

CROWN COPYRIGHT RESERVED

PLACES OF INTEREST ON THE ROUTE

Buckler's Hard

Charming and largely unspoilt 18th century 'street' leading down to the shores of the lovely Beaulieu River. Bucklers Hard was established in 1724 by the second Duke of Montagu, who intended it to become a sea port of consequence. Although this end was never achieved the Hard established itself for a while as a shipyard of some importance, and it was here that several ships-of-the-line that fought at Trafalgar were built....Agamemnon, Swiftsure, Illustrious and Euryalus. Its prosperity was short lived, but it has left a unique flavour lingering in this corner of the Forest.

The two terraces of mellow brick cottages face each other across a wide 'green', where ponies graze; and one can walk down to the quay, from whence there are boat trips down the river, or even across to the Isle of Wight. There is a hotel, the front of which is the exquisite 'Masters Builders House', and a Maritime Museum, which tells the story of Buckler's Hard most effectively.

Beaulieu Abbey

The Abbey was founded in 1204 by King John, whose original grant of seven thousand acres was eventually extended to no less than ten thousand. It is for this reason that this south eastern corner of the New Forest remains outside the bounds of the Crown Land. The Cistercian monks built a splended abbey at Beaulieu, and although largely robbed and destroyed, following its dissolution in 1538, the remains are well worth visiting.

The Great Gatehouse now forms part of the residence of Lord Montagu, and is known as Palace House, but the ruined Cloisters and Chapter House are delightful. There is an interesting museum in the Lay Brother's Refectory and the splendid Monk's Refectory now serves as the Parish Church

The National Motor Museum, etc.

This was built and is maintained by the National Motor Museum Trust, and houses a splendid collection of over two hundred historic cars, commercial vehicles and motor cycles, plus many interesting displays on almost every aspect of motoring history from 1895 to the present day.

The 'Beaulieu Complex' comprises not only the Motor Museum, but also Palace House and Gardens, Beaulieu Abbey itself (see above), and various special features including a high level Monorail which passes through the Motor Museum on its circuit of the grounds, a replica of a 1912 open-topped London bus which gives rides, 'Transporama' sound and vision presentation, a miniature veteran car ride and an outstanding model railway layout. There are also a number of shops and refreshment facilities and a visit here can easily extend over several hours.

Beaulieu Village, Exbury and Lepe

(See Page 11)

1. Buckler's Hard

2. Landing Stage at Buckler's Hard

3. Below Beaulieu Mill

4. Exhibits from the National Motor Museum outside Palace House, Beaulieu. (A National Motor Museum Photograph)

MAP 5

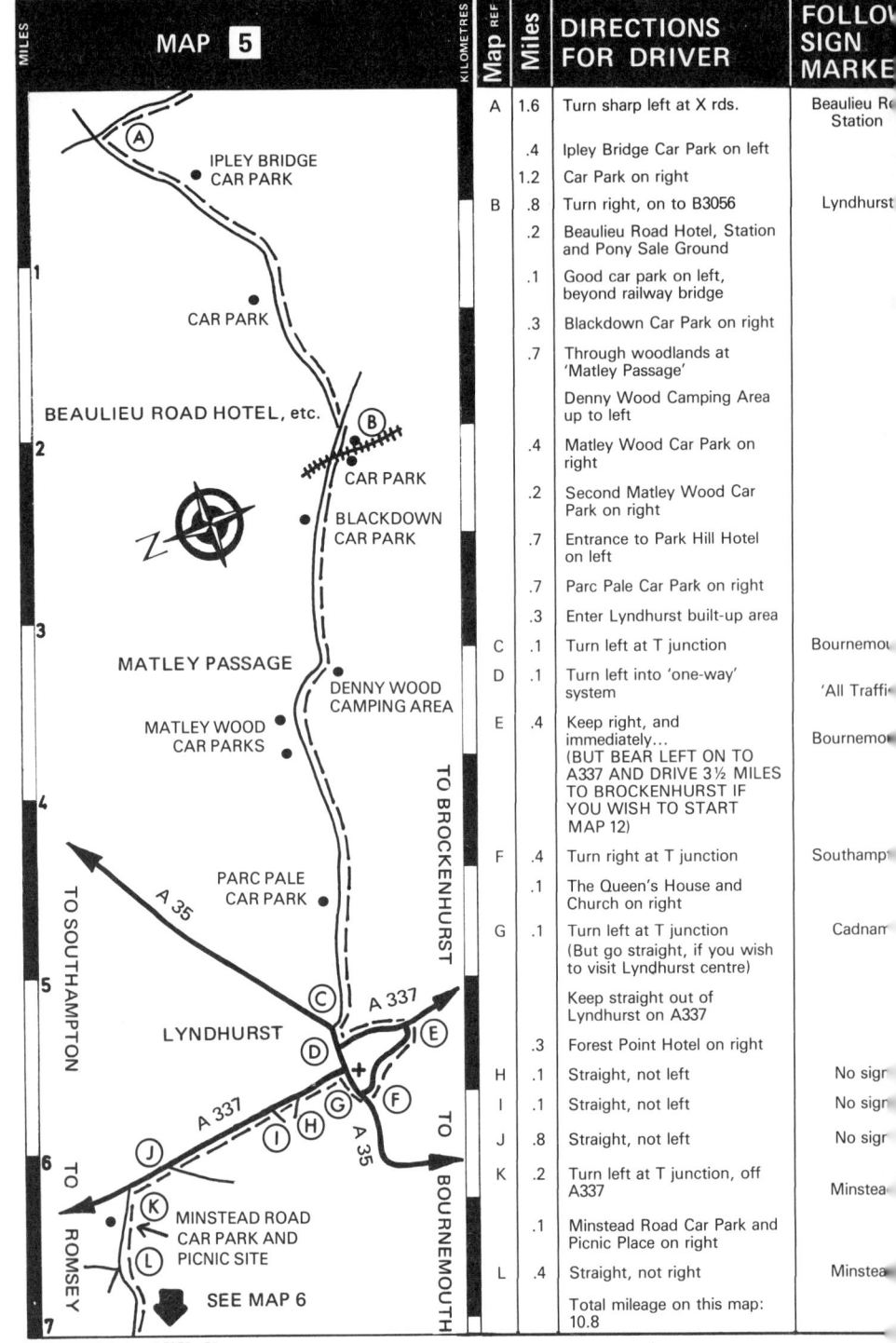

Map Ref	Miles	DIRECTIONS FOR DRIVER	FOLLOW SIGN MARKED
A	1.6	Turn sharp left at X rds.	Beaulieu Rd Station
	.4	Ipley Bridge Car Park on left	
	1.2	Car Park on right	
B	.8	Turn right, on to B3056	Lyndhurst
	.2	Beaulieu Road Hotel, Station and Pony Sale Ground	
	.1	Good car park on left, beyond railway bridge	
	.3	Blackdown Car Park on right	
	.7	Through woodlands at 'Matley Passage'	
		Denny Wood Camping Area up to left	
	.4	Matley Wood Car Park on right	
	.2	Second Matley Wood Car Park on right	
	.7	Entrance to Park Hill Hotel on left	
	.7	Parc Pale Car Park on right	
	.3	Enter Lyndhurst built-up area	
C	.1	Turn left at T junction	Bournemouth
D	.1	Turn left into 'one-way' system	'All Traffic'
E	.4	Keep right, and immediately... (BUT BEAR LEFT ON TO A337 AND DRIVE 3½ MILES TO BROCKENHURST IF YOU WISH TO START MAP 12)	Bournemouth
F	.4	Turn right at T junction	Southampton
	.1	The Queen's House and Church on right	
G	.1	Turn left at T junction (But go straight, if you wish to visit Lyndhurst centre)	Cadnam
		Keep straight out of Lyndhurst on A337	
	.3	Forest Point Hotel on right	
H	.1	Straight, not left	No sign
I	.1	Straight, not left	No sign
J	.8	Straight, not left	No sign
K	.2	Turn left at T junction, off A337	Minstead
	.1	Minstead Road Car Park and Picnic Place on right	
L	.4	Straight, not right	Minstead
		Total mileage on this map: 10.8	

CROWN COPYRIGHT RESERVED

PLACES OF INTEREST ON THE ROUTE

Beaulieu Village (See Page 8)
Crowded and busy with traffic, it is nevertheless a most attractive village, with many mellow brick cottages and shops. The level of the Monk's Mill Pond is controlled by a sluice close to the road and its reedy edges are overlooked by Palace House. Below the Sluice the Beaulieu River is tidal and in summer a few boats moored below the mill lend colour to the lovely sweep of water, curving seawards beneath the woods.

Exbury Gardens (See Page 8)
One of the finest woodland gardens in Britain, with 200 acres of trees and shrubs, and glorious views out over the Beaulieu River. See the naturalised bulbs in spring, and the rhododendrons and azaleas in early summer.

Exbury Church (See Page 8)
This was built in 1907, but contains a beautiful bronze memorial of a young soldier on a tomb chest, beneath the tower, by the sculptor Cecil Thomas.

Lepe (See Page 8)
A shingle bathing beach, with fine views across the Solent.... an excellent point for ship spotting. It was to here that Roman roads ran from Ringwood and Southampton, and there was probably a small 'ferry port' for the Isle of Wight.

Beaulieu Road Pony Sales
These sales take place at the Sale Yard (on our right) during August, September and October, and are colourful features of the Forest 'calendar',

Lyndhurst
The 'capital' of the New Forest, Lyndhurst is a flourishing little town, and an ideal centre for exploration. It is over busy with traffic at most times of the year, but still survives as a useful shopping town. The west end of the High Street is dominated by the tall spire of the 19th century Parish Church, which is itself built on a steep mound. Beyond it lies the beautiful 17th century Queen's House, administrative centre of the Forestry Commission's Deputy Surveyor of the New Forest, and also the location of the Verderer's Hall and Court Room. This is the scene of Verderer's meetings four or five times a year, and is a large finely panelled room. *(Only open to the public six times a year, when the Verderer's Court is in session. Notice giving dates displayed outside.)*

Minstead
Small village with a wide green overlooked by the delightfully titled 'Trusty Servant Inn'. This sign depicts a man with the head of a pig, the ears of an ass, and the feet of a stag, and is copied from an early 17th century painting in Winchester College. The inscription beneath is lengthy, but well worth reading.
Minstead Church lies up a little lane beyond the Trusty Servant and should on no account be missed. It has an 18th century brick tower, capped with a
continued on page 13

1. In Beaulieu Village

2. The Beaulieu River near Ipley Bridge

3. The Queen's House, Lyndhurst

4. Forest Ponies in winter

11

MAP 6

Map REF	Miles	DIRECTIONS FOR DRIVER	FOLLOW SIGN MARKED
	.1	Enter Minstead	
A	.5	Straight, not right. Just beyond the Trusty Servant Inn, at Minstead village green	
B	.1	Almost immediately turn left at T junction	Fleet Water
C	.4	Straight, not right (But turn right to visit Furzey Gardens)	No sign
D	.1	Fork left	No sign
E	.5	Turn sharp right on to busier road	No sign
F	.1	Straight over X rds.	No sign
G	1.4	Turn right on to A31	Cadnam
H	1.0	Turn left at T junction off A31	'Rufus Stone'
	.3	Rufus Stone on left	
		Car Park and Picnic Place on right	
	.2	The Sir Walter Tyrrell Inn on right	
	.5	Through ford	
I	.6	Turn sharp left at X rds. by the Bell Inn, on to B3078, in Brook hamlet, and . . .	No sign
J		Immediately fork left, keeping on B3078	Fordingbridge
K	1.5	Turn right at X rds.	Bramble H
	.8	Bramble Hill Hotel entrance on left	
L	.1	Fork left at entry to Bramshaw	No sign
M	.4	Bear left on to B3079	No sign
N	.1	Straight, not right	No sign
O	.2	Straight, not right	No sign
	.3	Bramshaw Church on right	
P	.6	Straight, not right	Landford
Q	.1	Turn left, off B3079, just before cattle grid WATCH FOR THIS WITH CARE	Nomansland
R	.5	Fork right at entry to Nomansland	No sign
S	.1	Straight over X rds., and pass to the left side of the Lamb Inn WATCH FOR THIS WITH CARE	'South La...'
T	.2	Turn left at T junction	'Lyburn R...'
U	.3	Straight, not left	No sign
V	1.6	Bear right at T junction by old chapel	No sign
W	.2	Bear left at T junction near the Cuckoo Inn	Redlynch
X	.9	Straight, not right	No sign
	1.2	Attractive little Gothick lodge on left Total mileage on this map: 14.9	

CROWN COPYRIGHT RESERVED

PLACES OF INTEREST ON THE ROUTE

Minstead *continued from page 11*

while pinnacle and golden weather vane. It has a pleasant 17th century timber framed porch sheltering a doorway some five hundred years older. Inside there is a little two-decker gallery in finely carved oak, and a three-decker pulpit. There are also two box pews, more like small rooms, one of which has its own fireplace. Sir Arthur Conan-Doyle, creator of Sherlock Holmes, is buried in the churchyard. Do not miss a visit to Furzey Gardens, with a 16th century cottage housing an art and craft gallery, standing in eight acres of delightfully laid out gardens.

The Rufus Stone

The stone was originally set up in 1745 at the legendary site of the death of William II. However it became so defaced by vandals that the present cast iron cover was added in 1841. The inscription reads:

'Here stood an oak tree on which an arrow shot by Sir Walter Tyrrell at a stag glanced and struck King William II, surnamed Rufus, on the breast, of which he instantly died on the second day of August Anno Domini 1100.'

While we shall never know if this account was correct, it is certain that Sir Walter took no chances and left for France without delay.

This is a 'place of pilgrimage' for most visitors to the New Forest and we lacked the courage to exclude it from our route.....but beware of crowds and the inevitable sense of anticlimax.

Brook

Pleasant hamlet with a stream, a large green and two attractive inns, The Bell and The Dragon.

Bramshaw

Long straggling village with a surprising number of pigs roaming the common land and roadside, which makes a change from the inevitable ponies found elsewhere. Bramshaw church stands on a steep knoll above the road, well to the north of the village. Its little brick tower resembles Minstead, but was built as late as 1829. The brickwork makes a pleasing contrast with the flint and stone of the earlier parts of the building. Inside there are two small galleries and a finely timbered roof. There is a memorial to seven men of the parish who went down with the Titanic.

Nomansland

A dull village, whose only redeeming features are a fine wide green on the edge of the woodlands, which we are now leaving for a time, and the attractive little Lamb Inn.

Hamptworth

A thinly spread hamlet with a severe Methodist chapel and a splendid little inn, with mellow brick and thatch....The Cuckoo.

Lover

Do not let the prettily thatched cottage in Gothick style at its entrance convince you that Lover deserves its endearing title. It is in fact a dull place with bungalows much in evidence.

1. Minstead Church

2. 'The Trusty Servant' Inn Sign

3. At the Rufus Stone

4. In Bramshaw Wood

5. The Cuckoo Inn, Hamptworth

MAP 7

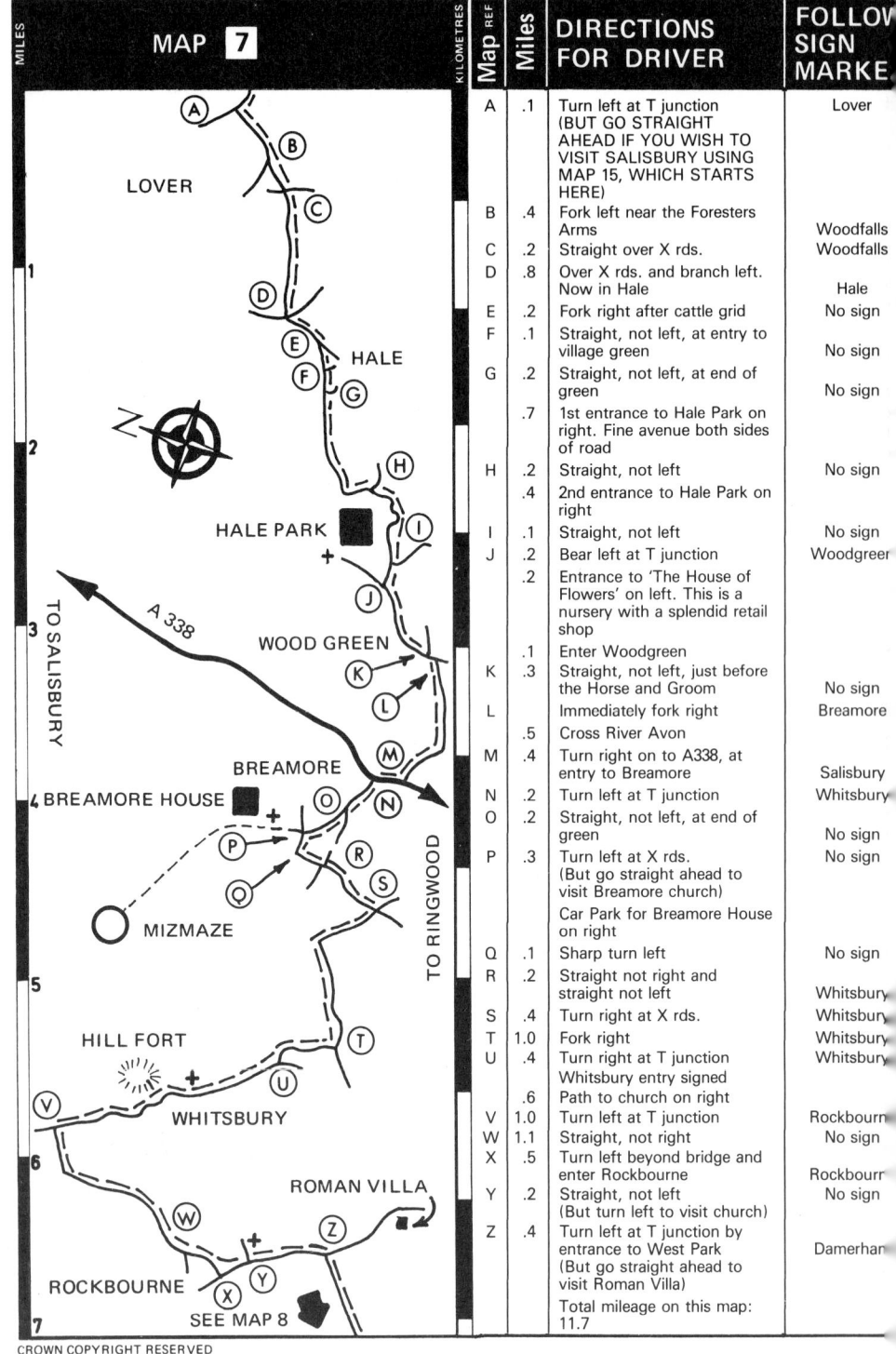

Map REF	Miles	DIRECTIONS FOR DRIVER	FOLLOW SIGN MARKED
A	.1	Turn left at T junction (BUT GO STRAIGHT AHEAD IF YOU WISH TO VISIT SALISBURY USING MAP 15, WHICH STARTS HERE)	Lover
B	.4	Fork left near the Foresters Arms	Woodfalls
C	.2	Straight over X rds.	Woodfalls
D	.8	Over X rds. and branch left. Now in Hale	Hale
E	.2	Fork right after cattle grid	No sign
F	.1	Straight, not left, at entry to village green	No sign
G	.2	Straight, not left, at end of green	No sign
	.7	1st entrance to Hale Park on right. Fine avenue both sides of road	
H	.2	Straight, not left	No sign
	.4	2nd entrance to Hale Park on right	
I	.1	Straight, not left	No sign
J	.2	Bear left at T junction	Woodgreen
	.2	Entrance to 'The House of Flowers' on left. This is a nursery with a splendid retail shop	
	.1	Enter Woodgreen	
K	.3	Straight, not left, just before the Horse and Groom	No sign
L		Immediately fork right	Breamore
	.5	Cross River Avon	
M	.4	Turn right on to A338, at entry to Breamore	Salisbury
N	.2	Turn left at T junction	Whitsbury
O	.2	Straight, not left, at end of green	No sign
P	.3	Turn left at X rds. (But go straight ahead to visit Breamore church)	No sign
		Car Park for Breamore House on right	
Q	.1	Sharp turn left	No sign
R	.2	Straight not right and straight not left	Whitsbury
S	.4	Turn right at X rds.	Whitsbury
T	1.0	Fork right	Whitsbury
U	.4	Turn right at T junction Whitsbury entry signed	Whitsbury
	.6	Path to church on right	
V	1.0	Turn left at T junction	Rockbourne
W	1.1	Straight, not right	No sign
X	.5	Turn left beyond bridge and enter Rockbourne	Rockbourne
Y	.2	Straight, not left (But turn left to visit church)	No sign
Z	.4	Turn left at T junction by entrance to West Park (But go straight ahead to visit Roman Villa)	Damerham
		Total mileage on this map: 11.7	

CROWN COPYRIGHT RESERVED

PLACES OF INTEREST ON THE ROUTE

Hale

Has a pleasantly wide open green overlooked by attractive cottages. The church lies close to the Avon, about a mile beyond the village, in the grounds of Hale Park. This handsome Georgian mansion looks out over the Avon valley towards the downlands beyond. It was built in 1715 by Thomas Archer the architect, for his own use, and modified in 1770 by Henry Holland. Do not overlook the church, which was re-built by Archer in 1717 and contains some excellent monuments.

Breamore

The centre of Breamore village is at the mercy of the busy Salisbury—Bournemouth road, but to the east there stands an old brick built mill house beside the clear waters of the Avon, while across the commonland to the west stands Breamore House and church.

Breamore church is one of England's outstanding Anglo-Saxon buildings. It probably dates from about A.D. 1000, and retains much of its original work. See especially the unique Anglo-Saxon inscription over the south transept arch, which in translation reads.....'Here the covenant is explained to you'; and the Anglo-Saxon sculpture of the crucifixion over the south doorway. The church is set in a delightful churchyard beneath the gaze of Breamore House, an Elizabethan mansion, which was largely re-built following a disastrous fire in 1856. However its setting beneath the downs is very pleasant, and it contains a fine collection of furniture and pictures. See also the Countryside Museum and the Carriage Museum.

Just over a mile to the north-west of Breamore House, by way of a footpath, lies the Miz-Maze, an interesting medieval (?) turf maze in the centre of a small wood.

Whitsbury

A 'thatch' village in a pleasantly wooded coombe overlooked by an Iron Age hill fort, Whitsbury Camp (Look right by the Manor Stud). The church was re-built in 1878, but it is well worth climbing the steep path by the little Post Office for the splendid views from the church, and for a glimpse of the handsome Georgian 'Old Rectory', set in its miniature park.

Rockbourne

Exceptionally pretty village with a clear chalk stream flowing beside thatched cottages and small flower gardens, and a low church built into the hillside above a beautiful manor house. See, in the church, the exquisite Flemish Triptyche, and the monument to Sir Eyre Coote, who fought with Clive at Plessey. (Monumental column in West Park, erected in his memory by the East India Company.)

Rockbourne Roman Villa (See Page 17)

1. Breamore House

2. South Porch, Breamore Church

3. Rockbourne Church

4. Summertime at Rockbourne

MAP 8

Map REF	Miles	DIRECTIONS FOR DRIVER	FOLLOW SIGN MARKED
A	1.1	Straight, not left, at entry to Damerham	Martin
B	.2	Turn left at T junction	Fordingbridge
C	.3	Turn right at T junction on to B3078	Cranborne
D	.1	Turn left at T junction off B3078	Lower Daggons
E	.2	Straight, not left (But walk down left to visit church. Possible by small car also)	No sign
F	.5	Straight, not left	No sign
G	1.1	Bear right at T junction	Crendell
H	.8	Turn right at T junction	Crendell
I	.8	Turn left at T junction in woods	Cranborne
J	1.0	Over small X rds. and immediately turn left on to B3078	Cranborne
	.5	Enter Cranborne	
K	.1	Over small X rds. and turn right at T junction	Wimborne Minster
L	.1	Turn left (But turn right, just beyond to visit church)	Wimborne Minster
M	.1	Straight, not left	Wimborne Minster
		Entrance to Manor House on right	
N	.1	Straight, not left, and immediately turn right off B3078	Handley
		Look down right for gorgeous prospect of Cranborne Manor	
O	.6	Turn left at T junction on to B3081	Wimborne St. Giles
P	.5	Straight, not left, at T junction, off B3081	Wimborne St. Giles
Q	.4	Straight, not left, at entrance to Wimborne St. Giles	No sign
		Church and almshouses on left	
R	.5	Straight, not right, by attractive village sign on right and stocks on left	No sign
S	.1	Fork left beyond stream	'The Gussage
T	1.2	Straight, not left (But turn left if you wish to visit Knowlton Church and earthworks, which lie 1 mile South East)	Gussage All Saints
		Total mileage on this map: 10.3	

CROWN COPYRIGHT RESERVED

PLACES OF INTEREST ON THE ROUTE

Rockbourne Roman Villa (See Page 14)
The excavated remains of a Roman Villa with a museum crammed with interesting exhibits, illustrating life in Roman Britain. We strongly recommend a visit here.

Damerham
A scattered village lying in the valley of the little River Allen. Its water meadows are overlooked by the church, built on rising ground away to the south-east. This dates back to the Norman period, although two medieval chapels have been demolished and the tower appears to have never been completed. See especially the small 'Christ in Majesty' over the south porch, and the Norman tympanum depicting a mounted knight spearing a grounded enemy (? St. George at Antioch).

Cranborne
Large unspoilt village which for centuries was the market town and centre of Cranborne Chase Court. The Chase once covered 700,000 acres and was administered in much the same way as a royal forest, a chase being 'a wild area set apart as a hunting preserve, its owner being a commoner as opposed to the Crown'.

Cranborne Manor, where the Chase Court sat, presided over by the owner, is a splendidly romantic building, which owes its present form to the conversion of a former hunting lodge in the 17th century. Its gardens are delightful, and are occasionally open to the public.

The fine church is mainly 13th century, although there is a Norman north doorway, and a large, well proportioned Perpendicular tower. There is a beautiful circular oak pulpit of the same period, and a series of gruesome wall paintings about a hundred years older.

Wimborne St. Giles
Delicious little village with church and almshouses overlooking a broad green, and beyond it, an attractive village sign. Close by flows the clear Allen stream, fresh from its water cress beds, and bound for the great park of St. Giles House. This is the 17th century mansion* of the Earls of Shaftesbury, and although its exterior has been heavily Victorianised, the interior retains the flavour of the 1750's, when it was extensively redecorated and re-furnished. There is also a remakable Shell Grotto of the same peroid.

The lovely mellow brick almshouses were built by the 1st Earl in 1624 and are almost joined to the Georgian church, which is probably the work of the famous John Bastard of nearby Blandford. Its exquisite interior was restored after a fire in 1908, and should on no account be missed.

*Not open to the public.

Knowlton Church and Earthworks
A ruined early Norman church standing inside the earthworks of a Bronze Age henge monument, about 1800 B.C. There are fine open views across the downland from this interesting and attractive little site. No other trace of Knowlton village remains.

1. At Rockbourne Roman Villa

2. Cranborne Manor

3. Church and Almshouses, Wimborne St. Giles

4. Church and Earthworks at Knowlton

MAP 9

Map showing route from Gussage All Saints through Moor Crichel, Crichel House, Witchampton, Tarrant Rawston, Tarrant Rushton, to Tarrant Keyneston. See Map 10.

Map Ref	Miles	DIRECTIONS FOR DRIVER	FOLLOW SIGN MARKED
A	.9	Straight over X rds. But turn right if you wish to visit Gussage All Saints church	Wimborne Minster
B	.2	Straight, not right	Horton
C	.3	Turn left at T junction	Moor Crichel
D	.2	Turn right at T junction	Moor Crichel
E	.3	Fork right	Moor Crichel
		Quaint lodge on right	
F	.4	Straight, not right	No sign
G	.4	Turn left at T junction	Witchampton
	.3	Crichel House visible over to left	
H	.2	Turn left at T junction	Witchampton
I	.6	Turn left at T junction	Witchampton
J	.2	Turn right at T junction	Witchampton
		Gates to Crichel House visible up left	
	.2	Enter Witchampton	
K	.2	Straight, not right, by village club	No sign
L	.2	Sharp turn right at T junction	'The Tarrants'
M	.3	Straight over X rds	Tarrant Rushton
N	.5	Straight over small X rds.	Tarrant Rushton
O	1.5	Bear left at T junction	'The Tarrants'
P	.4	Turn sharp right by airfield entrance	Blandford
Q	.3	Fork left	Blandford
R	.6	Straight, not right	Blandford
	.3	Bear left by large farm (But turn up right if you wish to visit Tarrant Rawston church . . . behind farm)	No sign
S	.4	Fork left	Wimborne Minster
T	.2	Straight, not left (Unless you wish to visit Tarrant Rushton village when you must turn left)	Tarrant Keynston
U	.8	Straight over X rds. at entry to Tarrant Keynston	Tarrant Crawford
	.6	Church on right	
		Total mileage on this map: 10.5	

CROWN COPYRIGHT RESERVED

PLACES OF INTEREST ON THE ROUTE

Gussage All Saints

Lies in a broad downland valley with its church overlooking a beautifully proportioned Georgian manor house, with a stream flowing beyond. The flint banded tower of the church is 14th century, and although the interior was over restored by the Victorians, it contains a Norman font of Purbeck marble and is worth looking at. The Earl Haigh Inn is not a very exciting looking building, but the delightfully named 'Amen Cottage', by the cross roads, is unashamedly and triumphantly 'picture-post card' in its appeal.

1. Amen Cottage, Gussage All Saints

Moor Crichel and Crichel House

An uninteresting estate village, whose predecessor was removed to give more scope to the builders of Crichel House. The original manor was burnt down in 1742, and it was this that gave impetus to the construction of the magnificent house and sweeping parkland, with its noble trees and great curving lake. It is possible that Thomas Archer (See Hale, page 15) was responsible for much of the original work, but the splendid dining room was almost certainly the work of the prolific James Wyatt. This has been described by Sacheverell Sitwell as one of the loveliest 18th century rooms, not only in England, but of the whole of Europe. Crichel is not open to the public.

2. Witchampton Church

Witchampton

One of East Dorset's most attractive villages, Witchhampton lies just to the west of the Allen stream, which is here crossed by a bridge, complete with a notice threatening anyone who harms it with transportation for life.....a relic of sterner times. There are many black and white thatched cottages and a long rambling stone manor house, which has several medieval details. The church stands opposite the manor, pleasantly situated above its sloping churchyard lawns. It was largely re-built in 1832, but still has a warmth of feeling about it. Do not miss the 17th century tablet, whose inscription includes the cheering lines . . . 'There's no rest like that within the urn'!

Tarrant Rawston Church

3. Our Road beyond Witchampton

Small cruciform 15th century church in a farmhouse garden, on the right after crossing stream between Points R and S. There is a Jacobean pulpit and a small west gallery, but it is worth visiting for its delightful situation alone.

Tarrant Rushton

The church looks out across the valley towards Tarrant Rawston, from its pleasant site amongst trees and well mown lawns. Like Rawston it is cruciform, but it is probably 200 years older. Its interior has been scraped, pointed and generally over restored, but it contains some well designed modern pews and an attractive memorial to the wife of Sir Alan Cobham, aerial showman of the thirties, and latterly, pioneer of re-fuelling aircraft in flight

4. Tarrant Rushton Church

Tarrant Keyneston (See page 21)

MAP 10

TARRANT CRAWFORD

SEE MAP 9

SHAPWICK

BADBURY RINGS

KINGSTON LACY HOUSE

TO DORCHESTER — A31

HOSP

WIMBORNE MINSTER

A 349

TO POOLE

SEE MAP 11

CROWN COPYRIGHT RESERVED

Map Ref	Miles	DIRECTIONS FOR DRIVER	FOLLOW SIGN MARKED
A	.7	Turn left at T junction	Spettisbury
	.3	Straight, not left, just before small bridge (Unless you wish to visit Tarrant Crawford)	No sign
B	.4	Turn left and immediately right, by new cross on old base	Shapwick
	1.1	Enter Shapwick	
C	.2	Turn left at X rds. by the Anchor Inn, and 2nd new cross on old base (But turn right if you wish to visit church ... .1)	Badbury Rings
D	.2	Straight, not right	No sign
	.2	Over offset X rds.	No sign
	.2	Wooded ramparts of Badbury Rings visible ahead	
E	.8	Turn right on to B3082	Wimborne
		Entry to Badbury Rings almost opposite. Fine avenue of trees lines the road from here to Kingston Lacy	
F	.7	Straight, not right	Wimborne
	.6	1st Kingston Lacy gates on right	
G	1.4	Straight over X rds.	Wimborne
H	.6	Fork right, keeping on B3082	Wimborne Minster
	.4	Enter Wimborne Minster Leper Hospital of St. Margaret on right, with medieval chapel	
I	.2	Turn left into 'One-Way' system by the Three Lions Inn	Ringwood
	.2	Bear left in town centre	Ringwood
J	.1	Turn right at T junction	Ringwood
K	.3	Bear right at Y junction at top of small hill	Ringwood
L	.2	Bear left	Ringwood
	.1	Over X rds. at traffic lights	Ringwood
		Total mileage on this map: 8.9	

PLACES OF INTEREST ON THE ROUTE

Tarrant Keyneston (See page 18)
A long, straggling village beside the cressy Tarrant stream, with an inn entitled 'The True Lovers Knot', and a dark church re-built in 1853, whose only redeeming features are a 15th century tower and a white painted south door.

Tarrant Crawford
This delightful little church lies half a mile from our route, but it is well worth the diversion (Beyond Point A..... See route details opposite). It is approached by an open road passing in front of a farmhouse, with a broad lawn, and a fine buttressed barn. The church is beside the Tarrant stream, and is a compact 12th and 13th century building. Its simple interior has been lovingly preserved and contains a wonderful series of 14th century wall paintings depicting the story of St. Margaret of Antioch.

In medieval times there was a small abbey of Cistercian nuns here and although this has vanished, there is evidence that King John's daughter, Joan of Scotland, was buried here.....also Bishop Poore, builder of Salisbury Cathedral.

Shapwick
Quiet village with several pretty thatched cottages and a most hospitable inn (The Anchor), where we lunched on the sort of bread and cheese we often dream about, but seldom run to earth. The church dates from Norman times and is built of stone and flint with mellow brick buttressing. It has an interesting interior, especially the north aisle chapel, but the little print hung in the church reveals how much was lost in the brutal 'restoration' of 1879.

The church is delightfully situated on the willow bordered banks of the Stour, not far from the Roman ford, on their road from Badbury Rings to Dorchester. In summertime you will find nesting swans in the reeds and cattle cooling off in the shallows. Ask in the Anchor Inn to hear the story of the Shapwick Monster and the 'Wheeloffs'.

Badbury Rings (N.T.)
Circular Iron Age Hill fort with three concentric ditches and banks, dominated by its high, wooded central area. Although it is difficult to appreciate its size from a distance, it covers 18 acres and is a mile around its outer perimeter. In Roman times it became the crossing point of two important roads (Bath – Hamworthy port, and Salisbury – Dorchester).

Now well restored by the National Trust, Badbury Rings provide some spectacular downland views, especially to the north.

Kingston Lacy House and Park (N.T.)
This is reached on our route by a glorious avenue of beech trees lining the B3082 road over the downs between Blandford and Wimborne.

Only opened by the National Trust in 1986, Kingston Lacy House was built by Sir Ralph Bankes in 1663–65, to replace the family home of Corfe

continued on page 23

Wimborne (See page 23)

1. View from Shapwick Churchyard

2. Our road near Badbury Rings

3. Kingston Lacy House (Photo. by T. P. Burr)

4. The Square, Wimborne Minster

MAP 11

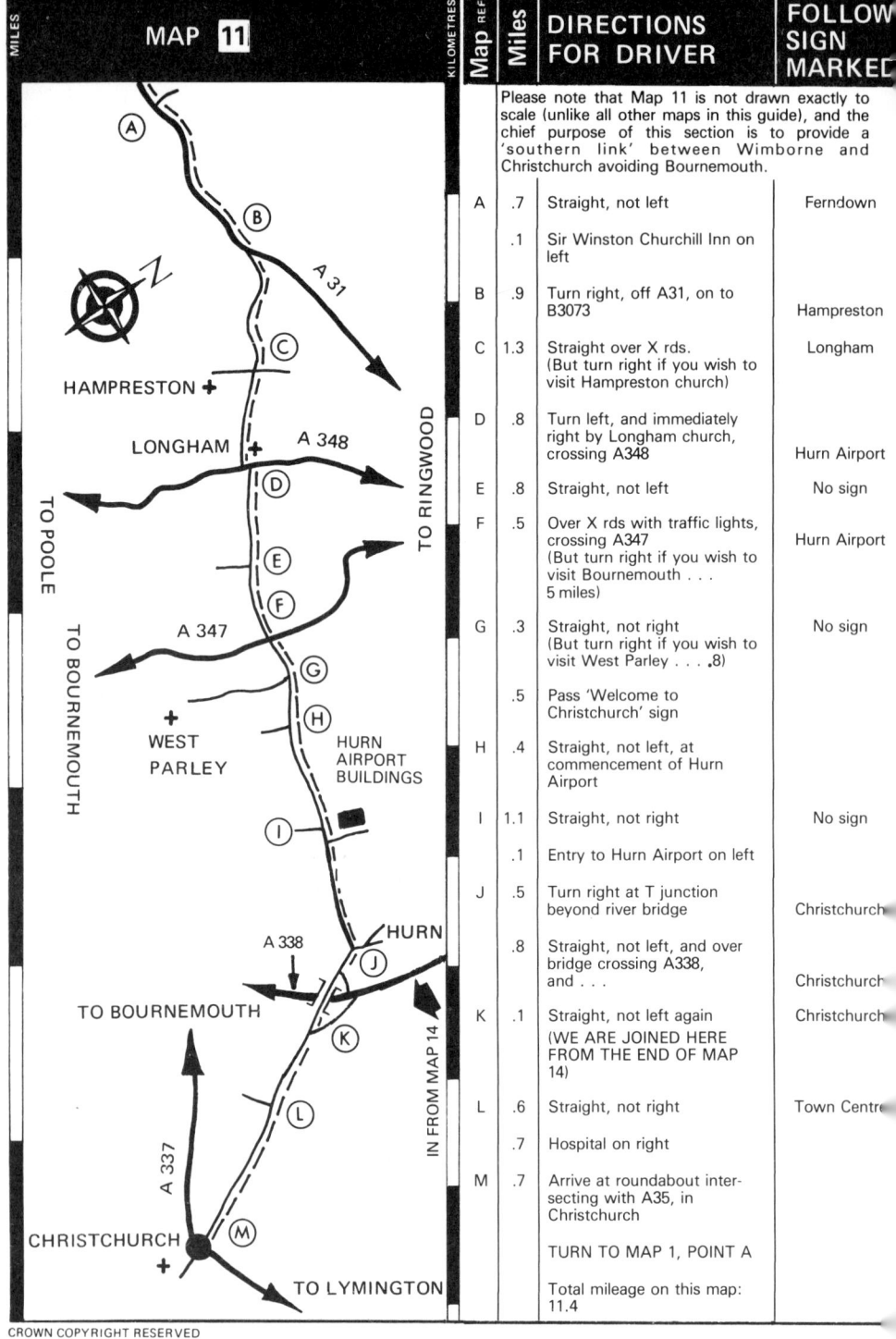

DIRECTIONS FOR DRIVER

Please note that Map 11 is not drawn exactly to scale (unlike all other maps in this guide), and the chief purpose of this section is to provide a 'southern link' between Wimborne and Christchurch avoiding Bournemouth.

Map REF	Miles	Directions for Driver	Follow Sign Marked
A	.7	Straight, not left	Ferndown
	.1	Sir Winston Churchill Inn on left	
B	.9	Turn right, off A31, on to B3073	Hampreston
C	1.3	Straight over X rds. (But turn right if you wish to visit Hampreston church)	Longham
D	.8	Turn left, and immediately right by Longham church, crossing A348	Hurn Airport
E	.8	Straight, not left	No sign
F	.5	Over X rds with traffic lights, crossing A347 (But turn right if you wish to visit Bournemouth . . . 5 miles)	Hurn Airport
G	.3	Straight, not right (But turn right if you wish to visit West Parley . . . .8)	No sign
	.5	Pass 'Welcome to Christchurch' sign	
H	.4	Straight, not left, at commencement of Hurn Airport	
I	1.1	Straight, not right	No sign
	.1	Entry to Hurn Airport on left	
J	.5	Turn right at T junction beyond river bridge	Christchurch
	.8	Straight, not left, and over bridge crossing A338, and . . .	Christchurch
K	.1	Straight, not left again (WE ARE JOINED HERE FROM THE END OF MAP 14)	Christchurch
L	.6	Straight, not right	Town Centre
	.7	Hospital on right	
M	.7	Arrive at roundabout intersecting with A35, in Christchurch	

TURN TO MAP 1, POINT A

Total mileage on this map: 11.4

CROWN COPYRIGHT RESERVED

PLACES OF INTEREST ON THE ROUTE

Kingston Lacy House *continued from page 21*
Castle, which had been dismantled by the Parliamentarians after his mother's heroically defended siege in the Civil War. This fine house, splendidly sited in a great park, was remodelled in 1835 by the versatile architect, Sir Charles Barry in neo-Renaissance style. Its contents include one of the finest private picture collections in the country, with works by Van Dyck, Lely, Titian, Rubens, Reynolds and Velasquez. The garden and park are also open to the public. At the time of writing it is intended that timed tickets will be issued to visitors to the house, to prevent overcrowding.

Wimborne Minster (See page 20)
Busy market town in the water meadows close to the Allen's meeting with the Stour. The town contains many pleasant 18th century houses, especially around the square, and in the streets leading into it. Wimborne's outstanding building of interest is the two towered Minster, which was built soon after the Conquest. The great Norman lantern tower carried a spire, until it collapsed in 1600, and the Perpendicular west tower was added in 1460. High up on the west tower is the famous Quarter Jack (1613), once a monk, but now a British Grenadier, who strikes the quarters on the bells either side of him.

The Minster's interior is most pleasing, and far too full of interest to be dealt with adequately here. It would be impossible to overlook the massive nave arcading or the central lantern tower, but look also for the astronomical clock, the chained library, and the Beaufort and Uvedale tombs (splendid examples of medieval and renaissance styles respectively).

Between the Minster and the Square will be found the excellent little 'Priest's House Museum', an early 16th century building with a wealth of local material imaginatively displayed, and a beautiful little garden at its rear.

In King Street, close to the main car park, is the Model Town, an exact replica of Wimborne, (compare photographs on Pages 21 and 23). This makes an excellent reward for younger children who have endured the rigours (in their opinion) of the Minster.

Hampreston
The mainly 15th century church has been over restored, but still retains some character. We liked the one 17th and several 19th century wall monuments.

Longham
Has an unusually distinguished 19th century Congregational church.

West Parley
Interesting small church close to the banks of the Stour, with attractive wood framed porch and some excellent 17th and 18th century woodwork. Well worth the diversion.

1. The Model Town, Wimborne

2. Longham Church

3. The Church Porch, West Parley

4. The Path to the Church, West Parley

5. Sunny cliffs at Bournemouth (A Jarrolds Photograph)

23

MAP 12

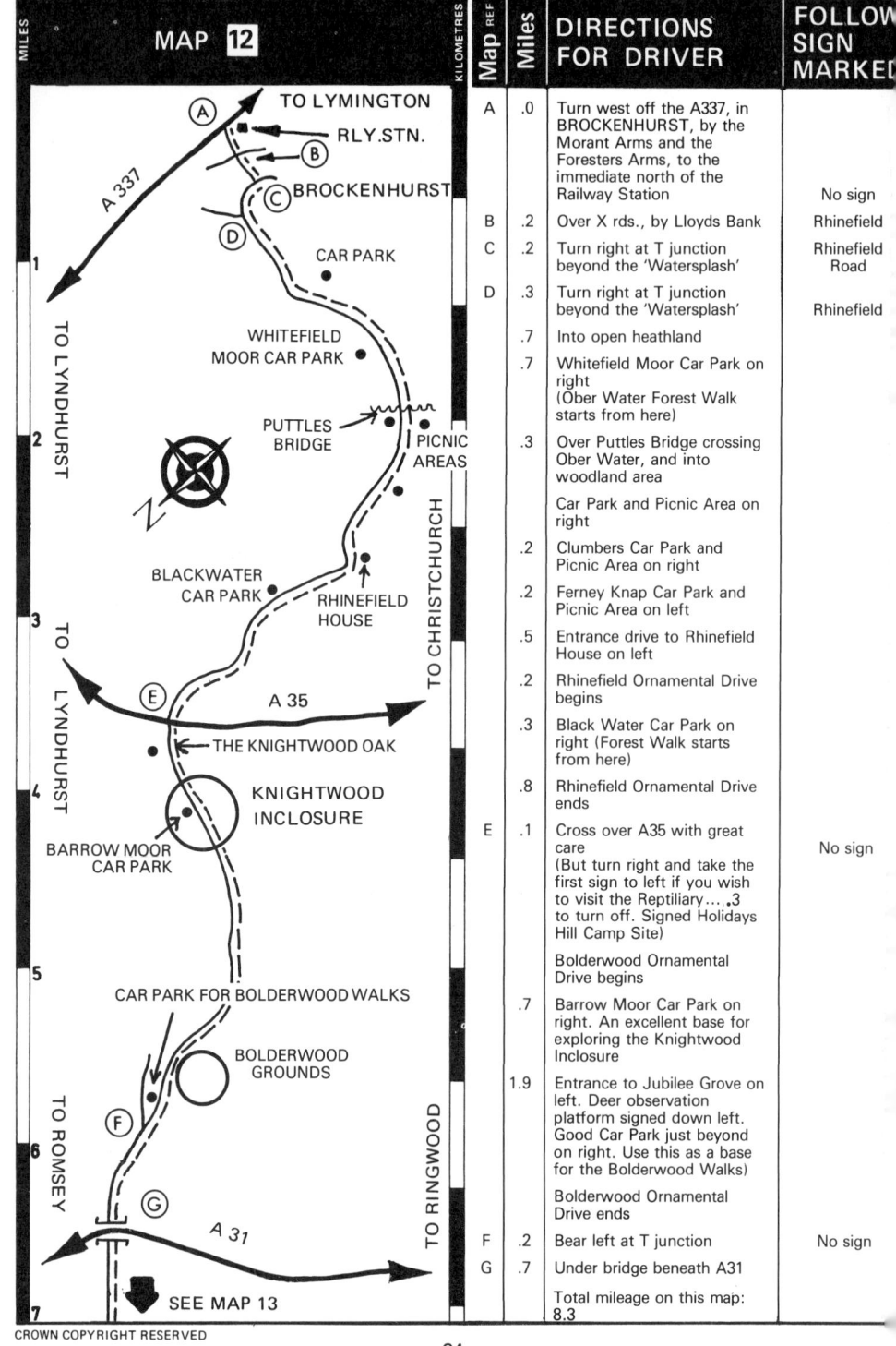

Map of Brockenhurst area

Locations shown on map:
- TO LYMINGTON
- RLY. STN.
- A337
- BROCKENHURST
- CAR PARK
- TO LYNDHURST
- WHITEFIELD MOOR CAR PARK
- PUTTLES BRIDGE
- PICNIC AREAS
- TO CHRISTCHURCH
- BLACKWATER CAR PARK
- RHINEFIELD HOUSE
- A 35
- THE KNIGHTWOOD OAK
- KNIGHTWOOD INCLOSURE
- BARROW MOOR CAR PARK
- CAR PARK FOR BOLDERWOOD WALKS
- BOLDERWOOD GROUNDS
- TO ROMSEY
- A 31
- TO RINGWOOD
- SEE MAP 13

CROWN COPYRIGHT RESERVED

DIRECTIONS FOR DRIVER

Map REF	Miles	DIRECTIONS FOR DRIVER	FOLLOW SIGN MARKED
A	.0	Turn west off the A337, in BROCKENHURST, by the Morant Arms and the Foresters Arms, to the immediate north of the Railway Station	No sign
B	.2	Over X rds., by Lloyds Bank	Rhinefield
C	.2	Turn right at T junction beyond the 'Watersplash'	Rhinefield Road
D	.3	Turn right at T junction beyond the 'Watersplash'	Rhinefield
	.7	Into open heathland	
	.7	Whitefield Moor Car Park on right (Ober Water Forest Walk starts from here)	
	.3	Over Puttles Bridge crossing Ober Water, and into woodland area	
		Car Park and Picnic Area on right	
	.2	Clumbers Car Park and Picnic Area on right	
	.2	Ferney Knap Car Park and Picnic Area on left	
	.5	Entrance drive to Rhinefield House on left	
	.2	Rhinefield Ornamental Drive begins	
	.3	Black Water Car Park on right (Forest Walk starts from here)	
	.8	Rhinefield Ornamental Drive ends	
E	.1	Cross over A35 with great care (But turn right and take the first sign to left if you wish to visit the Reptiliary... .3 to turn off. Signed Holidays Hill Camp Site)	No sign
		Bolderwood Ornamental Drive begins	
	.7	Barrow Moor Car Park on right. An excellent base for exploring the Knightwood Inclosure	
	1.9	Entrance to Jubilee Grove on left. Deer observation platform signed down left. Good Car Park just beyond on right. Use this as a base for the Bolderwood Walks)	
		Bolderwood Ornamental Drive ends	
F	.2	Bear left at T junction	No sign
G	.7	Under bridge beneath A31	
		Total mileage on this map: 8.3	

PLACES OF INTEREST ON THE ROUTE

Brockenhurst
A busy residential and holiday village, Brockenhurst has spread thinly over the surrounding heathland to the west of A 337, and is not over endowed with items of interest to visitors. The old church lies about a quarter of a mile to the south east of the level crossing, on the edge of Brockenhurst Park. Although it was one of only two New Forest churches mentioned in Domesday Book, it dates mainly from the 13th century. It has a brick built west tower, capped by a small shingle spire. *The touching gravestone of forest snake catcher 'Brusher' Mills is to be found beyond the church on the north side.

Rhinefield House
A late 19th century stone mansion with richly carved interiors and an attractive ornamental garden complete with a 'canal'...all set amongst trees similar to those beside the Rhinefield Ornamental Drive (see below).

The Rhinefield Ornamental Drive
A 'roadside arboretum' with colourful azaleas and rhododendrons, against a background of giant sequoias, Douglas firs, western red cedars, and any other trees exotic to the New Forest. Many of these are labelled and there are signed 'Forest Walks', leading from car parks at both ends of the Drive'. Read the interesting Forestry Commission leaflet describing both this and the Bolderwood Ornamental Drive (see below).

Holidays Hill Reptiliary
Drive through the Camp Site and the Reptiliary is by the Keeper's Cottage at the north end of the site. Here may be seen all the reptiles and amphibians of the New Forest.

Bolderwood Ornamental Drive
This two mile drive provides a splendid 'profile' of the different types of woodland found within the New Forest. Stop at Barrow Moor Car Park to visit the Knightwood Oak, an immense oak tree, with a girth of 22 feet at shoulder height, and which is probably over 800 years old.

Bolderwood Walks
There are three walks (all of which are described in another excellent Forestry Commission leaflet) which all start from the Car Park near the end of the Ornamental Drive...The Radnor Walk, the Mark Ash Walk, and the Bolderwood Arboretum Walk, the last of which incorporates a Deer Observation Platform. It is often possible to see wild deer at close quarters from here.

Continued from inside front cover.
Over the centuries small areas have been encroached upon, and Beaulieu was granted to the church; but apart from this, the Forest's pre-Norman pattern has survived to this day, with the grazing rights of the 'commoners',
Continued on page 27

---

1. Brockenhurst Church

2. Gravestone of 'Brusher' Mills, Brockenhurst

3. Ponies at Rhinefield Walk

4. Rhinefield House

5. The Rhinefield Ornamental Drive

25

MAP 13

Map REF	Miles	DIRECTIONS FOR DRIVER	FOLLOW SIGN MARKED
A	1.1	Straight, not right at T junction	Linood
	1.4	Road to High Corner Inn on right	
		Fine views to the right	
	.9	Linwood Caravan Park on right	
B	.1	Keep straight, not right, by the Red Shoot Inn	No sign
	.6	Pleasant valley with bracken covered slopes	
C	1.1	Turn right at X rds. by oak tree, and cross small ford	North Gorle
		Straight, not left, just before . . .	Mockbegga
	.1	Moyles Court (Manor House School) on left	
D	.6	Turn left at X rds.	Ibsley
E	.7	Turn right at T junction by Ibsley church on to A338	Fordingbrid
	.1	Old Beams Restaurant on right	
F	.2	Turn left at T junction, off A338 and . . .	Harbridge
		immediately cross River Avon	
	.5	Harbridge rectory and church on right	
G	.1	Bear left well beyond church	Alderhol
H	.7	Turn sharp left	Somerley
		Open woodlands now on both sides of road.	
	1.7	Entering Ringwood Forest (not signed)	
		Total mileage on this map: 9.9	

CROWN COPYRIGHT RESERVED

PLACES OF INTEREST ON THE ROUTE

Docken Water Ford (See Point C)
Delightful little ford with grassy banks, near large oak tree. However beware of crowds in high summer.

Moyles Court
A beautiful 17th century mellow brick manor house, with stables that look older, but may be of the same period. (Now a school, but may be viewed by appointment.) In 1685 the 70 year old, widowed owner of the house, Dame Alicia Lisle, gave shelter to two fugitives from Sedgemoor, and was condemned to be burned at the stake, by Judge Jeffreys, at Winchester Assizes. However local opinion was so outraged that the sentence was reduced to death on the block, and this was carried out at Winchester on 2nd September 1685. So much for 'the good old days'!

Ibsley
Small village astride the busy A 338, with a fine three arched bridge over the Avon, and a tree shaded weir beyond. The little church was built in 1832 but contains an attractive 16th century monument to Sir John Constable and his wife. This is decorated with a vine which not only sprouts grapes, but also the heads of Sir John's five children.

Harbridge
Appears to consist only of a church and rectory, but these two buildings are attractively set close to a small bridge on the edge of the Avon water meadows, complete with prosperous looking cattle and flower bordered streams. The west tower with battlements and corner turret is medieval, but the rest was re-built in 1838.

Continued from page 25
dating back to Saxon times, and jealously watched over during sessions of the ancient Verderers Court, now located in the Queen's House at Lyndhurst.

Forestry. The Forest came under the care of the Forestry Commission in 1924, but it was as early as the 17th century that the requirement for timber (and consequent profit to the royal owners), became more important than the hunting. However the Verderers Court, representing both the 'commoners' and (more recently) the wider interests of the public, have ensured that despite the demands of the ship builders and the depredations of two world wars, the Forest's varied beauty has remained largely intact.

Exploring the Forest. It is to the credit of the Forestry Commission that this splendid area has increased its productive output without detracting from the enjoyment of its many visitors. It is crossed by many excellent roads, but to gain most enjoyment do leave your car at one of the many good car parks provided and walk across heathland and into the deep woodlands. Until you do this you may feel that
Continued on page 28

1. At Docken Water Ford

2. Moyles Court

3. Ibsley Bridge

4. Rectory and Church at Harbridge

MAP 14

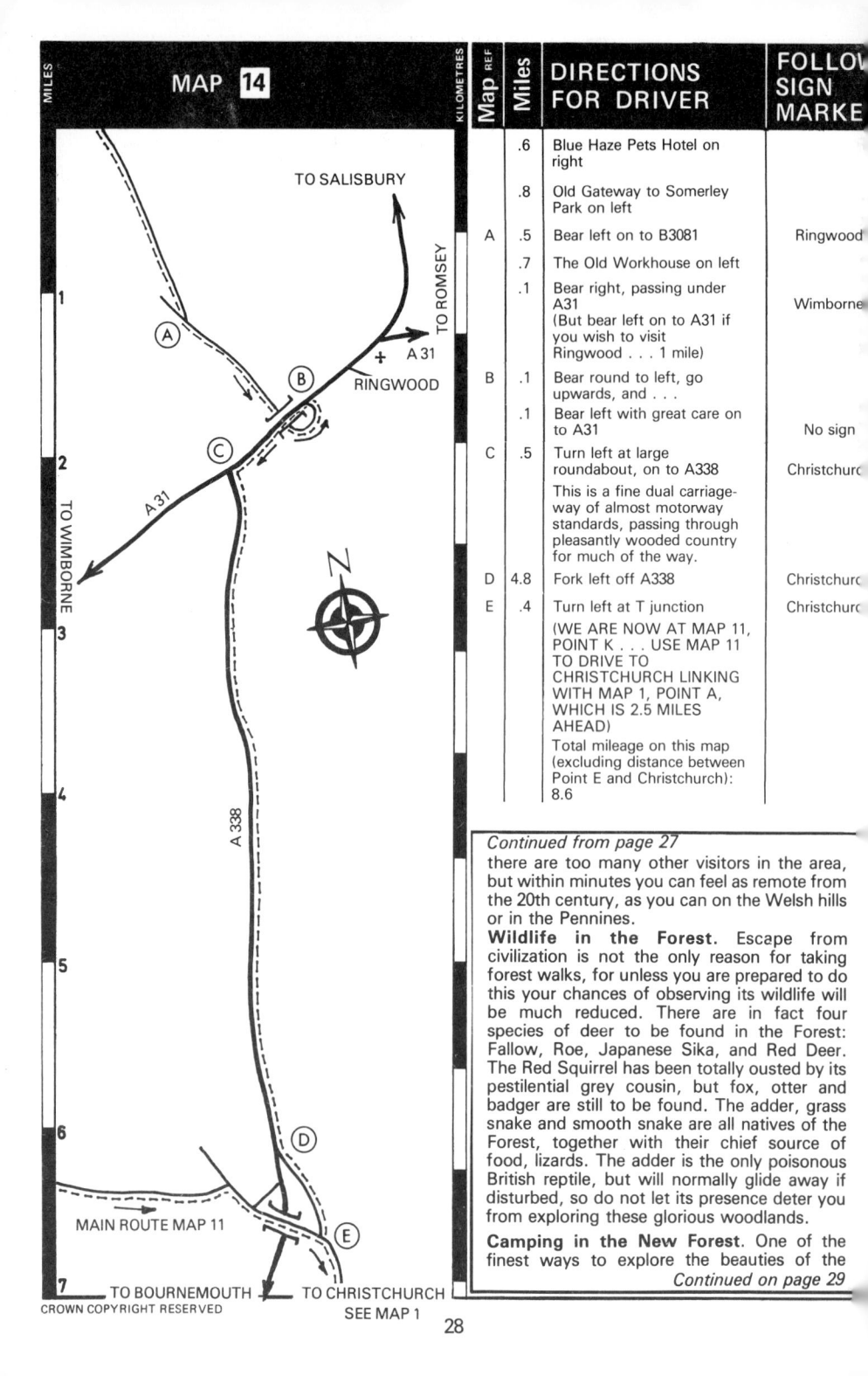

Map REF	Miles	DIRECTIONS FOR DRIVER	FOLLOW SIGN MARKED
	.6	Blue Haze Pets Hotel on right	
	.8	Old Gateway to Somerley Park on left	
A	.5	Bear left on to B3081	Ringwood
	.7	The Old Workhouse on left	
	.1	Bear right, passing under A31 (But bear left on to A31 if you wish to visit Ringwood . . . 1 mile)	Wimborne
B	.1	Bear round to left, go upwards, and . . .	
	.1	Bear left with great care on to A31	No sign
C	.5	Turn left at large roundabout, on to A338. This is a fine dual carriageway of almost motorway standards, passing through pleasantly wooded country for much of the way.	Christchurch
D	4.8	Fork left off A338	Christchurch
E	.4	Turn left at T junction (WE ARE NOW AT MAP 11, POINT K . . . USE MAP 11 TO DRIVE TO CHRISTCHURCH LINKING WITH MAP 1, POINT A, WHICH IS 2.5 MILES AHEAD) Total mileage on this map (excluding distance between Point E and Christchurch): 8.6	Christchurch

Continued from page 27

there are too many other visitors in the area, but within minutes you can feel as remote from the 20th century, as you can on the Welsh hills or in the Pennines.

Wildlife in the Forest. Escape from civilization is not the only reason for taking forest walks, for unless you are prepared to do this your chances of observing its wildlife will be much reduced. There are in fact four species of deer to be found in the Forest: Fallow, Roe, Japanese Sika, and Red Deer. The Red Squirrel has been totally ousted by its pestilential grey cousin, but fox, otter and badger are still to be found. The adder, grass snake and smooth snake are all natives of the Forest, together with their chief source of food, lizards. The adder is the only poisonous British reptile, but will normally glide away if disturbed, so do not let its presence deter you from exploring these glorious woodlands.

Camping in the New Forest. One of the finest ways to explore the beauties of the
Continued on page 29

PLACES OF INTEREST ON THE ROUTE

Ringwood (Turn left beyond the Old Workhouse)
Busy market town beside the River Avon, with several pleasant 18th century buildings. The large church was re-built in the 1850's and is attractively grouped with the mellow brick Old Vicarage and a stuccoed 18th century building overlooking the Market Square. The interior of the church is attractively furnished with blue carpets and a nave altar dressed in Portugese tapestry of light contemporary design. There is a good 15th century brass commemorating John Prophete, the last Rector of Ringwood, who later became Dean of Hereford.

The daily round in Ringwood appears to have made few concessions to the holidaymaker, and for this reason it has a genuine flavour, since lost to some of its more 'popular' neighbours.

Continued from page 28
Forest is to camp or caravan in the specially selected sites set aside for this purpose by the Forestry Commission. The Camping Season is usually from the Thursday before Good Friday or 1 April whichever is the earlier. Details are contained in a leaflet obtainable from the Information Caravan situated in the Car Park at Lyndhurst.* Permits are available on site. The number of people taking advantage of the camping facilities has steadily increased over the recent years and facilities receive heavy pressure at the peak holiday periods. For this reason you are advised to camp at off peak times to enjoy the forest to the full.
*The camp site Information points, during the season or Queen's House, Lyndhurst, out of season.

The New Forest Ponies. These most attractive animals are as much a part of the Forest as the woods and pastures over which they graze. They were certainly here long before William's afforestation, although breeding improvements over the last 200 years have considerably altered their appearance. Some ponies are turned out for summer grazing only, but there are probably over a thousand that run in the Forest throughout the year. They are the property of individual commoners and most mares and foals restrict their grazing to an area no more than a mile or so from one point. Stallions however wander more freely. By ancient right ponies have precedence over all wheeled traffic, and will often be found wandering in village streets, or across main roads; so please take care, especially at night.

These ponies are found in a wide range of colours, and to see a group of mares and foals, chestnuts, strawberry roans, blacks and dark browns, quietly grazing beneath the sunlit trees in summertime is to experience the very essence of the Forest.

1. The Open Forest

2. Ringwood Church

3. The Old Workhouse, Ringwood

4. Inside Christchurch Priory

5. Quiet Moorings at Christchurch

MAP 15

Map REF	Miles	DIRECTIONS FOR DRIVER	FOLLOW SIGN MARKED
		Starting from Map 7, Point A, which is common with Point A on this Map.	
A		Straight, not left at T junction	Downton
B	.5	Over X rds.	Downton
	.6	Enter Redlynch	
C	.1	Over small X rds. by the Kings Head	'Bowers Hil
D	.1	Turn right at X rds. on to B3080	Downton
E	.2	Over small X rds.	No sign
	.3	Entry to Downton signed	
F	.4	Straight, not left	No sign
G	.2	Turn right at X rds.	Standlynch
	.1	Downton church on left	
H	1.0	Straight, not right, at T junction	No sign
	.6	Trafalgar House just visible through trees on left	
I	.6	Bear left at T junction	No sign
	.6	River Avon visible in valley to left	
		Spire of Salisbury Cathedral visible ahead left	
	1.6	Alderbury entry signed	
J	.2	Bear left at T junction, near entry to Longford Park (PRIVATE)	'Shute End Road'
	.1	Longford Castle visible over to left	
K	.5	Straight, not right at Y junction	No sign
L	.3	Bear left on to the 'old A36'	No sign
	.5	Bear left on to the new A36	Salisbury
	.5	'City of Salisbury' entry signed	
M	.9	Bear left at 1st roundabout	'City Centre
N	.4	Turn right, round 2nd rounadabout	'City Centre
O	.4	Turn left by the White Hart Hotel	'Cathedral
P	.2	Turn left at traffic lights (But at peak times, turn right and follow signs to main car park)	'Cathedral
Q	.2	Arrive at car parking area in the Cathedral Close	
		Total mileage on this map: 11.1	

CROWN COPYRIGHT RESERVED

PLACES OF INTEREST ON THE ROUTE

Redlynch
Straggling village with considerable development on its fringes. It has two small Victorian churches and several pleasant thatched cottages...but is not a very memorable place.

Downton
Attractive village on the River Avon. Its western half is fringed by the busy A338, but between here and the bridge, lies the 'Borough', with wide greens, thatched cottages, and a pleasant inn. Above the bridge stands the Tannery, its red brick front almost hidden by lush Virginia creeper, and looking down to cottages below the weir. The large flinty church is cruciform and has a brick parapet to the aisles. The lovely medieval south door and doorway are protected by a 17th century porch, and inside there is an interesting series of sculptured capitals. Do not miss the very handsome 18th century monuments in the chancel and the south transept.

Trafalgar House
Dignified Georgian mansion dating from 1773, and originally called Standlynch. It was presented in 1814 to Nelson's heirs, whose descendants lived here until recently. The 'Ganges Room' is panelled with timber from the ship of the line of the same name, and there are fine views over the Avon valley. *(Not open to the public.)*

Alderbury
Away from the busy A36, Alderbury has an undisturbed air, and looks across the Avon valley to Longford Castle, amongst the trees. The little Victorian church lies opposite Alderbury House, a Georgian building, which incorporates much stone taken from Salisbury Cathedral during Wyatt's 'restoration' in 1789.

Longford Castle*
A fascinating triangular mansion, built by Sir Thomas Gorges between 1575 and 1591, whose final touches were paid for with treasure from the wreck of a Spanish galleon off Hurst Castle. Although extensively altered in the 18th and 19th centuries Longford retains a splendid atmosphere, and is rich in interior decoration, furniture and paintings. The River Avon flows beneath its walls, and adds colour to the park, which was laid out by the inevitable 'Capability' Brown. (*Not open to the public.*)

Salisbury
Description of this splendid cathedral town requires far more space than we can provide here, but may we suggest that you park your car as soon as possible and spend several hours wandering on foot, to absorb its delightful atmosphere. Naturally you will gravitate towards the mighty spired cathedral, but pause awhile on the broad lawns of the close, with its surrounds lined by a fascinating series of houses and buildings of many periods.

And so, into the cathedral itself...where you must consider your New Forest journey complete, and a new journey of discovery about to commence.

1. Below the Tannery at Downton

2. The North Gate, Salisbury

3. Salisbury Cathedral from Harnham Mill

4. The Cloisters, Salisbury Cathedral

INDEX

	Page
Alderbury	31
Allen, River	17, 19, 23
Archer, Thomas	15, 19
Avon, River	3, 15, 27, 29, 31
Badbury Rings	21
Bankes, Sir Ralph	21
Bastard, John	17
Beaufort Tomb	23
Beaulieu Abbey	7, 9
Beaulieu Road	11
Beaulieu Village	11
Bolderwood Arboretum	25
Bolderwood Ornamental Drive	25
Bolderwood Walks	25
Boldre	5
Bournemouth	3
Bramshaw	13
Breamore	15
Breamore House	15
Brockenhurst	25
Brook	13
Brown, Capability	31
Buckler's Hard	7, 9
Burley	5
Christchurch	3
Cobham, Sir Alan	19
Colebourne, Charles	7
Coleridge	3
Conan-Doyle, Sir Arthur	13
Constable, Sir John	27
Constable's House	3
Coote, Sir Eyre	15
Corfe Castle	23
Courtenay Chapel	7
Cranborne	17
Cranborne Chase	17
Cranborne Manor	17
Crichel House	19
Damerham	17
Deer Observation Platform	25
Docken Water	27
Downton	31
Exbury Church	11
Exbury Gardens	11
Fawley Refinery	8
Flambard, Bishop	3
Furzey Gardens	13
Gilpin, William	7
Gorges, Sir Thomas	31
Great Coxwell	7
Gussage All Saints	19

	Page
Hale	15
Hale Park	15
Hampreston	23
Hamptworth	13
Harbridge	27
Hengistbury Head	3
Holidays Hill Reptiliary	25
Holland, Henry	15
Holmes, Sherlock	13
Hood, H.M.S	7
House of Flowers	14
Hurn Airport	22
Hurst Castle	31
Ibsley	27
Isle of Wight	7, 9, 11
Jeffreys, Judge	27
Joan of Scotland	21
John, King	9, 21
Kempe, John	7
Kingston Lacy	21, 23
Knightwood Oak	25
Knowlton	17
Lepe	11
Lisle, Dame Alicia	27
Longford Castle	31
Longham	23
Lover	13
Lymington	7
Lymington River	5
Lyndhurst	11
Maritime Museum	9
Mark Ash Walk	25
Master Builder's House	9
Matley Passage	10
Minstead	11, 13
Miz-Maze	15
Model Town, Wimborne	23
Montagu, Lord	9
Moor Crichel	19
Moyles Court	27
Mudeford	3
National Motor Museum	9
Nelson	31
Nomansland	13
Ober Water Walk	25
Otterwood Gate	8
Palace House	9
Poore, Bishop	21
Priest's House Museum	23
Quarter Jack	23
Queen's House	11

	Page
Radnor Walk	25
Redlynch	31
Reptiliary	25
Rhinefield House	25
Rhinefield Ornamental Drive	25
Rhinefield Walk	25
Ringwood	29
Rockbourne	15
Rockbourne Roman Villa	17
Rufus Stone, The	13
Rufus, King William	3, 13
Rysbrack	7
St. Giles House	17
St. Leonards	7
Salisbury	31
Salisbury Cathedral	21, 31
Sedgemoor	27
Scott, Sir Walter	3
Shaftesbury, Earls of	17
Shapwick	21
Sitwelll, Sacheverell	19
Solent	7
Sopley	3, 5
Sowley Pond	7
Stour, River	3, 21
Sway Tower	5
Tanners Lane	7
Tarrant Crawford	21
Tarrant Keyneston	21
Tarrant Rawston	19
Tarrant Rushton	19
Tarrant Stream	21
Thomas, Cecil	11
Titanic, The	13
Trafalgar	9
Trafalgar House	31
Tregonwell, Squire	3
Trusty Servant Inn	11
Tyrrell, Sir Walter	13
Uvedale Tomb	23
Verderers' Hall	11
Vicar's Hill	7
West Park	15
West Parley	23
Whitsbury	15
Wimborne Minster	23
Wimborne St. Giles	17
Winchester	27
Witchampton	19
Woodgreen	15
Wyatt, James	19, 31